BRITISH RAILW

PAST and PRESENT

No 52

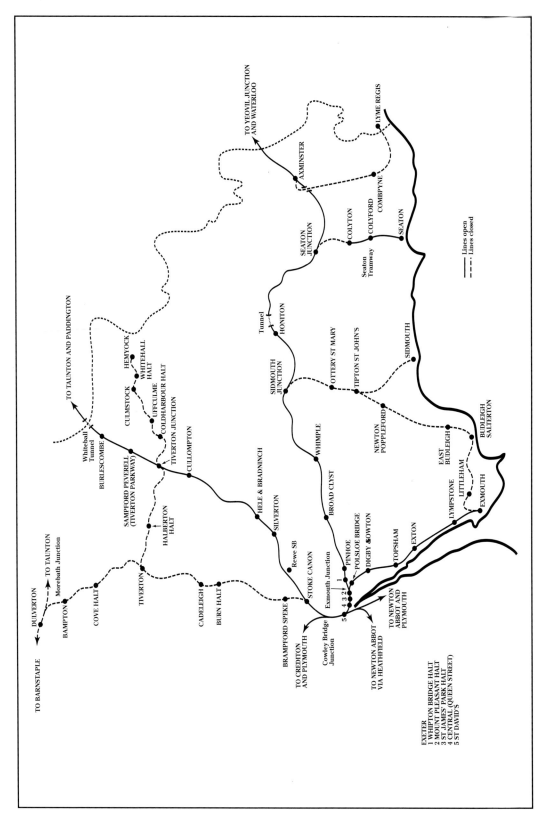

Map of the area covered by this book, showing locations featured or referred to in the text.

BRITISH RAILWAYS

PAST and PRESENT

No 52

East Devon

David Mitchell

Past and
Present

Past & Present Publishing Ltd

First published in 2005
Reprinted 2008

British Library Cataloguing in Publication Data

A catalogue record for this book is available from the British Library.

ISBN 978 1 85895 211 6

Past & Present Publishing Ltd
The Trundle
Ringstead Road
Great Addington
Kettering
Northants NN14 4BW

Tel/Fax: 01536 330588
email: sales@nostalgiacollection.com
Website: www.nostalgiacollection.com

Printed and bound in the Czech Republic

HONITON: The original station buildings on the London & South Western Railway's route into Devon were designed by architect Sir William Tite and featured tall chimneys and highly pitched gables in a Gothic style. At Honiton the main buildings were situated on the down side and featured an ornate canopy valance.

They were demolished in the 1970s and replaced by a featureless flat-roofed structure, but this was subsequently modified to include an apex roof that also provides limited shelter for waiting passengers. *Terry Gough/DHM*

CONTENTS

MOUNT PLEASANT HALT: Looking towards Exmouth Junction, Standard 5MT 4-6-0 No 73110 *The Red Knight* passes the site of the halt as it cruises down the 1 in 100 grade towards Blackboy Tunnel with the 1.5pm Waterloo to Exeter Central train on Saturday 22 July 1961.

Undergrowth and security fencing prevent the taking of an exact facsimile in 2005. In this more elevated view from 11 November 1998, No 37891 is working a rake of stone wagons. They had been emptied from the siding on the far left of the yard. *R. A. Lumber/DHM*

INTRODUCTION

At its maximum, the railway network of Devonshire extended to about 500 miles, with more than 200 passenger stations and halts open; the original volume in this series covering the whole county (No 8 *Devon*, ISBN 1 85895 058 9) only included 79 of them. It is therefore planned to take a more detailed look at the county's railways in the pages of three further books, enabling many new locations to be given the 'past and present' treatment. Additionally a fresh look can be given to most of the places featured the first time around, usually with a different angle of view to that seen previously. No photographs will be duplicated from the original book during this process.

A broadly anti-clockwise journey will be taken around the county; starting in this book with a look at the former Southern lines in the east, before studying the Great Western's legacy in the Exe and Culm Valleys. The second volume will cover North and West Devon, and the journey will end by featuring the Plymouth area before heading through the south of the county back towards Exeter.

In the 15 years since the original book was compiled, East Devon's railway network has remained stable, with no lines or stations closing. One new station, Digby & Sowton, has been opened during this period.

The big change that has occurred is, of course, the privatisation of the network, and the complexities that this has brought to the system. Very few of those in favour of the basic idea appear to support the structure that evolved at the time, particularly the separation of the infrastructure from operations. No fewer than four different companies currently operate the passenger services within this area. The Waterloo to Exeter service was the first to be privatised, and is operated by South West Trains. After some initial difficulties this service continues to perform satisfactorily, serving seven stations featured in these pages. To an extent this is due to the operator inheriting the modern Class 159 DMU fleet from BR, albeit that this train is not entirely appropriate for inter-city travel. Unfortunately any expansion of services on this successful line will be difficult due to the extensive singling of the route undertaken in 1967. Recent analysis has suggested that services could be transformed by investing £22.7 million in infrastructure improvements, including two passing loops at Axminster and Whimple. To re-instate double track over the whole route has been costed at £160 million!

The Great Western service from Paddington to the West was secured by a management buy-out, but has since been taken over by First Group. The admirable HST fleet still covers most of the services, but it is now getting old, with the earliest sets rapidly approaching their 30th birthdays. It is disappointing that there are as yet no firm proposals for the fleet's replacement, although at the time of writing new engines are being tested with a view to further refurbishment. The Exmouth branch and certain other local services are operated by Wessex Trains. This company is based in Exeter and has been particularly active in promoting its services in the local community. However, this franchise is due to be combined with the Great Western one, and when this happens there has to be a real fear that interest will wane in the loss-making branches. The Exmouth branch provides an invaluable service, particularly taking commuters into Exeter. Some 878,000 journeys were recorded in 2004, and it does now seem hard to believe that it was proposed for closure in the Beeching Report.

The cross-country franchise was awarded to Virgin Trains and virtually all services are now operated by its fleet of new 'Voyager' trains. I will refrain from any further comment!

It is sad to report that currently no rail freight traffic originates within the area covered by this title. The only incoming traffic carried by rail is fuel to Wessex's Exeter depot, and aggregates to a distribution depot in Riverside Yard. Traffic lost since the original book was compiled includes scrap metal, timber, coal and cars. The current state of affairs is reflected in the fact that the remaining staff at Riverside are being made redundant. Plans are in place for a new intermodal depot near Broad Clyst, and this does offer some hope for the future.

No preserved standard gauge railways operate within East Devon, but the Seaton Tramway goes from strength to strength and provides a thoroughly enjoyable ride beside the River Axe. In addition, a railway centre has been established at the former Cadeleigh station, giving the opportunity to enjoy narrow gauge and miniature railway rides at this Exe Valley location.

In my Introduction to the original book, I commented on how difficult it had been to take many of the 'present' photographs, due to locations becoming totally overgrown. Unfortunately this has only worsened in the intervening years, and many of the modern scenes herein feature rampant growth, and not just on the closed lines! Coupled with building development and Network Rail's predilection for erecting palisade fencing, it is becoming more difficult with the passage of time to replicate the exact viewpoint of the archive pictures. Once again I have often elected to record a slightly different perspective, to enhance the interest in today's views. The majority of these photos were taken in the last year or so specifically for the book; but I have also dipped into my own archive to include views that are either no longer accessible, or to add some variety to the trains depicted. I hope that this approach is acceptable to the reader.

As always, this book would not have been possible without the efforts of those photographers who recorded the 'past' for their own pleasure, but who are now prepared to share the fruits of their efforts with many others. I am most grateful to them and to the landowners who granted me permission to enter their private property. My thanks also go to Eric Youldon for information, and for his comments on the captions.

David Mitchell, Exeter

BIBLIOGRAPHY

Cooke, R. A. *Atlas of the GWR* (Wild Swan, 1988)
   Track Layout Diagrams of the GWR, Section 15 (R. A. Cooke, 1979)
Gough, Terry and Mitchell, David *BR Past & Present No 29 Dorset* (Past & Present, 1996)
   BR Past & Present No 44 Dorset – A Second Selection (Past & Present 2004)
Maggs, Colin G. *Rail Centres: Exeter* (Ian Allan, 1985)
   Railways to Exmouth (Oakwood, 1980)
Maggs, C. and Paye, P. *The Sidmouth, Seaton & Lyme Regis Branches* (Oakwood, 1979)
Messenger, Michael *The Culm Valley Light Railway* (Twelveheads, 1993)
Mitchell, David *BR Past & Present No 8 Devon* (Past & Present, 1991)
   BR Past & Present No 30 Somerset (Past & Present, 1996)
Mitchell, Vic and Smith, Keith *Yeovil to Exeter* (Middleton, 1991)
   Branch Line to Lyme Regis (Middleton, 1987)
   Branch Lines to Seaton & Sidmouth (Middleton, 1991)
   Branch Lines to Exmouth (Middleton, 1992)
   Taunton to Exeter (Middleton, 2002)
   Branch Lines Around Tiverton (Middleton, 2001)
Owen, John *The Exe Valley Railway* (Kingfisher, 1985)
Phillips, Derek and Pryer, George *The Salisbury to Exeter Line* (OPC, 1997)
Pryer, G. A. *Track Layout Diagrams of the SR, Section 5* (R. A. Cooke, 1982)
Vaughan, Adrian *The West of England Resignalling* (Ian Allan, 1987)

Axminster to Exeter Central

AXMINSTER: The LSWR route from Yeovil Junction to Exeter opened to passengers on 19 July 1860, the line following the Axe Valley into Devon with Axminster the first station in the county. 'S15' Class 4-6-0 No 30824 has arrived with the 10.37am train from Exeter Central to Templecombe on 8 July 1961. Visible above the engine is the station water tank, that drew its supplies from the River Axe. Immediately behind the camera is a bridge carrying the A373 into town, the down platform extending under this bridge via a narrow access point.

   The station is now the only one open between Crewkerne and Honiton, a distance of some 23 miles; and thus serves as an important railhead for the area. On 7 May 2005 DMU No 159013 is departing as the 0820 Waterloo to Exeter St David's service. *Terry Gough/DHM*

AXMINSTER: Also on 8 July 1961, 'U1' Class No 31901 passes the 30-lever signal box as it enters the station with the 10.42am Exmouth/11.07am Sidmouth to Cleethorpes train comprised of ER stock. On its right is the bay platform constructed to serve the Lyme Regis branch for its opening in August 1903. The branch climbed from here at 1 in 80 around a curve to a bridge over the main line, and then away to the south.

The signal box closed on 5 March 1967 when all track in the station other than the main running lines was taken out of use. In 1992 the down platform was extended past the site of the box, allowing the closure of the eastern section of the original platform from under the road bridge; the current platform can handle a six-coach train. All Waterloo trains stop here, but not the 1010 Paignton to Portsmouth and Brighton (comprised of Nos 159012/002), which is speeding eastwards on 7 May 2005. *Terry Gough/DHM*

AXMINSTER: Adams '0415' Class 4-4-2T No 30584 is attaching through coaches from Lyme Regis to a Waterloo train on 13 August 1960. The foreground track forms part of the substantial goods yard. At one time a small engine shed was located behind the camera, housing a locomotive used for banking trains to Honiton; but this was demolished in about 1903.

The yard closed to goods traffic in April 1966 and the area is now occupied by several businesses. However, the portion seen in the foreground was disued in May 2005; as No 159022 departed as the 0920 service from Waterloo to Plymouth. It will shortly pass Axminster's renowned carpet factory. *Terry Gough/DHM*

SEATON JUNCTION station opened with the line as Colyton for Seaton, and was re-named Colyton Junction in 1868 when the Seaton branch opened. It was reconstructed in 1927/8 with two through roads for non-stopping trains and long loops provided to serve the extended platforms. Rebuilt 'Merchant Navy' Class 'Pacific' No 35030 *Elder Dempster Lines* is on the up through road with the 2.25pm Plymouth to Waterloo train on 8 August 1960, passing the impressive LSWR bracket with its lower-quadrant semaphore arms. This tall signal was provided as a driver's view through the station was obscured by two footbridges; the lower repeating arms were for the drivers of stopping trains.

The station closed with the branch on 7 March 1966. The platforms remain but are becoming overgrown, while the main buildings on the up side also survive in commercial use. The 1Z14 0743 Bournemouth-Exeter-Salisbury track-recording train makes its return journey on 30 March 2004, top-and-tailed by Nos 37109 and 37042. *Terry Gough/DHM*

SEATON JUNCTION was given its final name in July 1869. 'West Country' 4-6-2 No 34036 *Westward Ho* streaks towards the station with what is probably the 1.45pm Ilfracombe and Torrington to Waterloo train, at 4.35pm on 28 June 1958. Considerable milk traffic originated from an Express Dairy Depot that adjoined the up platform – hence the six-wheel tank wagons standing in the up sidings. The 55-lever signal box came into use in April 1928 when it replaced the original 1875 structure. To the left of this is the 'new' branch platform that was provided as part of the rebuilding. Previously a bay platform had been used, requiring branch trains to reverse both on arrival and departure.

By Wednesday 20 August 1969 the signal box had been demolished and much track removed. Class 42 diesel-hydraulic No D866 *Zebra* is running over the former down through road, which was retained as the main running line when the route was singled in 1967. The track next to the down platform is out of use, while the up through line now forms part of a loop providing access to the residual sidings. Although these still contain milk tanks, the factory has closed and the 'Warship' is actually hauling its loaded tank from the creamery at Chard Junction to Exeter.

In August 1972 the running line was slewed to join the up through line and today these are the only rails remaining. On 2 April 2005 Nos 43026 and 43021 power the 0804 Penzance to Paddington HST. This train is being diverted due to track being relayed in the Cullompton area. All these photographs were taken from a long concrete bridge that carries a public footpath over the site of the station. *Peter W. Gray/R. A. Lumber/DHM*

WILMINGTON: From Seaton Junction the railway climbs between the Axe and Otter Valleys for more than 7 miles, with a gradient of 1 in 80 for nearly all of the final 4½ miles. This overbridge, on a minor road close to the village of Wilmington, is about halfway up the incline, and in May 1964 Bulleid 4-6-2 No 34020 *Seaton* is required to put in some effort with the 3.5pm Salisbury to Exeter Central stopper, despite its light load.

On 9 July 1999 the 7Z07 0755 Eastleigh to Exeter Riverside weed control train, top-and-tailed by Nos 37065 and 37679, is spraying as it climbs. *Derek Frost/DHM*

WILMINGTON: Turning the other way, and only 4 minutes later at 5.25pm, the photographer was able to record another 'Pacific', No 34060 *25 Squadron*, as it charges downhill with the 4.30pm Exeter Central to Waterloo train. Honiton Incline signal box was situated a little further west on the steepest part of the bank; it was a block post controlling a crossover, with catchpoints to divert any runaways into a refuge siding.

On 7 June 2005 No 159005 speeds through the 'jungle' forming the 1235 Paignton to Waterloo service. *Derek Frost/DHM*

CLEAVE: On 15 April 1965 'West Country' No 34026 *Yes Tor* has plenty of steam to spare as it drifts down Honiton bank with an up freight. Out of sight around the curve at the rear of the train is the 1,345-yard-long Honiton Tunnel, the longest on the LSWR, its western portal marking the summit of the incline. The loco is passing an allotment, once a common feature of the lineside, and something to give the horrors to today's Health & Safety Executive!

On 5 May 1980 No 33028 is working the 1428 Exeter St David's to Waterloo. This class worked most services over the route from September 1971, but were largely replaced by Class 50s just one week after this photo was taken. A visit here in April 2005 revealed the location to be relatively unchanged – just a little more overgrown! *J. H. Bamsey/DHM*

HONITON: Another of the original stations was located in this town, famous for its lace-making. When the line opened it was single track throughout, with passing loops provided at all the stations. With increasing traffic it soon became necessary to double sections of the route, the whole line being completed by July 1870. In addition to longer-distance stopping trains, Honiton was served by commuter services from Exeter. On Saturday 23 November 1963 Ivatt 2MT 2-6-2T No 41320, built by BR to an LMS design in 1952, is arriving with the 1.50pm train from Exeter Central. The loco will run round its stock and shunt it into the down sidings before returning to Exeter light engine.

On 7 June 2005 Nos 159016/007 arrive with the 1210 Exeter St David's to Waterloo service. *Derek Frost/DHM*

HONITON: At 2.15pm on Tuesday 30 March 1965 Standard 3MT 2-6-2T No 82030 pauses with the 1.52pm Axminster to Exeter Central stopper. This train was the last regular steam passenger turn from Exmouth Junction shed. The original 1875 signal box had stood in the foreground until replaced in June 1957, and the goods shed and yard are to the right.

It is not possible to stand in the same position today as a large Building Supplies Centre occupies the site. However, by peering over a fence at the west end of this structure on 5 October 2004 it was possible to record No 67014 passing with a track inspection train. The 'new' signal box is still used to control a passing loop and a surviving refuge siding on the up side. The down line is signalled for bi-directional operation, allowing up trains to access the down platform for passengers' ease, when no westbound trains are being crossed. *R. A. Lumber/DHM*

SIDMOUTH JUNCTION station was named Feniton when it opened in 1860, referring to a village less than a mile away. Suffering something of an identity crisis, it was renamed Ottery Road in July 1861, then Ottery St Mary in April 1868, the latter being a town some 3 miles away. Finally it was branded Sidmouth Junction in 1874 when the branch opened. Pictured from a minor road leading to Feniton, No 34095 *Brentor* arrives at 12.8pm on Saturday 27 June 1964 with the 8.35am Waterloo to Ilfracombe and Plymouth train.

On 2 April 2005 another diverted HST will be a relatively unusual caller at what is now once again called Feniton as it slows with the 1205 Paddington to Penzance service (power cars Nos 43139/165). *Derek Frost/DHM*

SIDMOUTH JUNCTION: Also on 27 June 1964, but looking in the opposite direction from the same bridge, another 'light Pacific', No 34079 *141 Squadron*, is leaving at 10.51am with the 8.10am Ilfracombe/10.28am Exeter Central to Waterloo train. Standard 4MT 2-6-4T No 80039 can be glimpsed on the Sidmouth branch, which curves away to the south just above the 'Pacific'. On the left are two sidings; a turntable had been located between these and the branch until its removal in about 1930.

Two Class 159s, Nos 159012/010, pass the (obscured) milepost 159 on 9 May 2005, departing with the 1010 Exeter St David's to Waterloo service. The 159s have worked the vast majority of the scheduled services over this line since 1993. *Derek Frost/DHM*

SIDMOUTH JUNCTION: 'West Country' No 34013 *Okehampton* arrives at 4.00pm on 25 July 1964 with the 3.35pm stopper from Exeter Central to Yeovil Town. The train is passing over a level crossing located at the west end of the station, which was controlled from a small gate box on the Exeter side of the crossing. The main signal box was positioned beyond the east end of the up platform. On the right of the train is a large brick-built waiting shelter, with the main buildings on the opposite platform. Behind the camera is the branch bay platform.

The station closed with the branch from 6 March 1967 and all its buildings were demolished. However, the village of Feniton was expanding with extensive residential development immediately north of the railway, and local pressure led to the station re-opening under its original name on 3 May 1971, with the former down platform reinstated on the now single-track railway. Shortly after a heavy downpour, No 159012 is reflected in this platform as it arrives with the 13.30 Exeter to Waterloo service on 5 October 2004. *R. A. Lumber/DHM*

WHIMPLE station also featured the work of architect Sir William Tite. The main buildings were located on the up side, with a typical small hipped-roof waiting shelter on the other platform. Now preserved 'West Country' No 34092 *City of Wells* is on the 9.35am Yeovil Town to Exeter Central train on Sunday 12 April 1964. Peeping out from behind the main building is a monkey-puzzle tree, a well known feature of the station.

Although public goods services ended here from 4 December 1967, the goods yard was retained for traffic to and from the Whiteways Cider factory, originally established here in 1892. On 11 August 1978 BR Sulzer Type 2 No 25225 has brought in two empty vans, and after shunting the yard is about to return to Exeter Riverside with a loaded wagon and brake-van in tow. *R. A. Lumber/DHM*

WHIMPLE: Cider production ended here in 1989, and when the main line was relayed in July 1990 the up road and sidings were disconnected and lifted. Two years later a £117,000 improvement scheme included reconstruction of the up platform; a shortened section was raised and extended forward over the old up formation to meet the surviving rails. This work is seen in progress on 24 October 1992.

The down platform, waiting shelter and footbridge were demolished in November of that year. The main buildings survive as a dwelling. *Both DHM*

WHIMPLE: When Absolute Block signalling was introduced to the route in 1875, signal boxes to a standard design were erected at all the stations. Although some of these were later replaced, others lasted for a very long time, such as that at Whimple, which survived into the diesel area; the 0813 Salisbury to Exeter DMU arrives at 1007 on Saturday 3 June 1967.

However, it was not to last much longer, as closure came only a week later when the line was singled. At that time the down road was retained as the running line and passengers had to use the footbridge for all services. As we have seen, though, the up track was retained to provide access to the goods yard, with ground frame operation. The gutter in the middle of the new platform marks the approximate original extent of the original as the 1550 Paignton to Honiton service departs on 7 May 2005. *R. A. Lumber/DHM*

BROAD CLYST, another of the line's original stations, was located about a mile south of the village from which it takes its name. The up yard was occupied by the civil engineers in 1896, with expansion of the facilities in 1929. This permanent way pre-assembly depot can be noted ahead of 'U' Class 2-6-0 No 31798 as it pauses with the 11.12am Exeter Central to Salisbury train on Saturday 9 December 1961. The signal box roof can be spotted above the loco, with the down yard and goods shed on the right. An 0-4-0 diesel shunter (No DS1169) worked in the permanent way depot from 1959 to 1964, and can be glimpsed in the distance with a tall water tank behind.

The depot closed at the end of 1964 and a supermarket now stands on its site. The goods shed survives in commercial use, but is hidden in April 2005. Industrial units have been built between it and the station. *R. A. Lumber/DHM*

BROAD CLYST station's main buildings were located on the down platform, which was shorter than its up counterpart, and at 7.46pm on 1 August 1965 they are passed by 'West Country' No 34005 *Barnstaple* with the 7.35pm Exeter Central to Salisbury train. This was a regular surviving steam working that summer.

Goods facilities were withdrawn from the following month and the passenger service ceased on 7 March 1966. The remaining building is occupied as offices by several companies, but some evidence of the down platform is visible on 30 April 2005 as No 159011 passes with the 1210 Exeter St David's to Waterloo service. A new town is planned for the area and this will have a station just to the east of here. *R. A. Lumber/DHM*

PINHOE: At 1858 on Saturday 10 June 1967 Class 42 No D868 *Zephyr* passes the single siding that comprised the goods yard. It is the last day of double-track working, and from 2200 that night a 25-hour possession will start to allow completion of Stage 3 (Final) of the singling scheme, covering the Chard Junction to Pinhoe section. A new single to double line connection will be provided here, and tools are neatly laid out in the foreground in readiness for this work. The 'Warships' were the main motive power over this route from August 1964 to September 1971.

The siding had already been taken out of use in the previous month, and the area was subsequently used by a coal merchant, but was unoccupied on 7 November 2004 when Nos 159012/008 passed forming the 1003 Waterloo to Paignton service. *R. A. Lumber/DHM*

PINHOE: The signal box was another of the original 1875 structures and was located just to the west of the goods yard, adjacent to a level crossing. Originally containing an 11-lever frame, it was extended to 17 in 1943 when a crossover and sidings were installed just to the west of the station to serve a Ministry of Food Cold Store. English Electric Type 4 No 50009 *Conqueror* speeds past at 1235 on 22 August 1983 with the 0910 Waterloo to Exeter St David's service.

The box was the last original one to see service on this line; surviving until 13 February 1988, when operations were switched to Exmouth Junction's cabin. It has entered well-earned preservation, however, and is now located at Bere Ferrers station on the Gunnislake branch. On 9 June 2005 Nos 159010/021 approach forming the 1020 Waterloo to Exeter St David's service. *Both DHM*

PINHOE station opened on 30 October 1871, more than ten years after the line. It was adjacent to its namesake village and more than 2 miles from Exeter. Due to its later construction, it was provided with non-standard buildings. At 7.31pm on Monday 8 July 1963 'S15' Class 4-6-0 No 30832 is arriving on the 5.34pm Templecombe to Exeter Central stopping train.

The village became part of Exeter in 1966, the once open countryside between the two places having been replaced by urban sprawl. This development was of no benefit to the station, however, as it closed on 7 March that year, unable to compete with bus and car. However, it was re-opened on 16 May 1983 to cater for an expanding population. Steam locomotives still occasionally pass through, such as Standard 5MT 4-6-0 No 73096 with the 0834 Wimbledon to Exeter 'Cathedrals Express' on 7 November 2004. The only surviving original building, now a house, is visible on the left. *R. A. Lumber/DHM*

PINHOE: About 25 chains west of the station a siding served the Pinhoe Grain Silo. It is not clear when this was installed, but it has been reported that it was not used for grain traffic from 1946 until August 1974 when, after some track upgrading, trainloads of French maize for cattle feed began arriving via the Zeebrugge to Harwich ferry. On 12 February 1977 the sidings are full with Polybulk hoppers as 'Hastings' DEMU No 1034 passes forming the Saturdays-only 1357 Exeter St David's to Brighton service. This was a diagrammed working for these units from 1972 until 1977.

Until 1965 another line led off this siding to serve a brickworks, then from March 1982 occasional wagon-loads of bricks were loaded at the silo. On 18 April 1983 No 31231 is reversing two empty wagons into the siding; after loading they will be tripped to Riverside Yard, then forwarded to Grangemouth in Scotland.

The brick traffic ended within a year or two, the grain flow having already ceased. The siding was taken out of use on 6 December 1987 and the silo was in course of demolition on Sunday 12 February 1989 as No 50001 *Dreadnought* passed with the 1227 Exeter St David's to Waterloo train. The loco is in Network Southeast livery, the route having become part of that sector in 1986.

The brickworks dominates the background on 16 May 2004 as the 1000 Plymouth to Paddington HST passes by, but as with so many other industries its products are no longer carried by rail. The train is being diverted due to work inside Whiteball Tunnel. *All DHM*

PINHOE: The brickworks and silo are still prominent as we continue our westward journey on the outskirts of Exeter. Standard 4MT 2-6-0 No 76008 is working the 1.45pm Yeovil Junction to Exeter Central service at 3.56pm on Saturday 11 July 1964.

A graphic illustration of how largely unchecked growth has been allowed to affect the lineside is provided on 5 January 2005 as EWS's Canadian-built No 66218 passes the same spot with a returning route-learning trip from Yeovil Pen Mill to Exeter. *Derek Frost/DHM*

WHIPTON: Once another rural agricultural area, this became a busy suburb of Exeter, not least due to the presence of the LSWR's Exmouth Junction complex, which was located within the parish, and was the area's major employer. We can see the grain silo in the left background as No 34023 *Blackmore Vale* forges west with the 11.30am Brighton to Plymouth train at 4.14pm on 11 July 1964. It will shortly pass the site of Whipton Bridge Halt, one of three such halts opened in Exeter's suburbs in 1906 when a railmotor local service was introduced between Queen Street station and Honiton; the halt had closed in January 1923.

On 3 January 2005 GBRailfreight's 'Shed' No 66708 and Electro-Diesel No 73204 provide a most unusual sight on this line as they haul 'Thumper' DEMUs Nos 205032/028 to their new home on the Dartmoor Railway, running as the 5V84 0825 Tonbridge West to Meldon Quarry service. *Derek Frost/DHM*

EXMOUTH JUNCTION SHED: The LSWR originally had a small engine shed at Queen Street station, but the site was not suited for development, and a larger depot was opened in November 1887 on a 'green-field' site near the junction for the Exmouth branch. Unfortunately the building was not substantial enough and the metalwork was soon subject to corrosion. With the need for an even larger building, it was decided to replace it with a new concrete structure with components from the nearby concrete works. The new shed was built to the rear of the old one, which had to be kept in use, sections only being demolished when parts of the new building could be brought into use; for that reason construction took from 1924 to 1929. For many years the depot had an allocation of Drummond's handsome 'T9' 4-4-0s, and No 30715 was recorded 'on shed' at 2.45pm on 20 March 1954. The higher roof of the repair shed on the left was to accommodate a travelling gantry crane.

After demolition in 1970, the site of the shed lay derelict until 1979 and the erection of a supermarket. Further comment is superfluous! *J. H. Bamsey/DHM*

EXMOUTH JUNCTION SHED: The 'new' depot was one of the largest on the Southern Railway, with an allocation of about 110 locos and well over 500 men employed in the shed and the nearby Carriage & Wagon shops and concrete works. With the loss of traffic and dieselisation, the allocation gradually declined until the shed closed to steam on 1 June 1965. It remained open for a while servicing diesels, and on 8 January 1966 it was visited by No 34015 *Exmouth*, which is backing off shed after being turned and serviced while working a special train – the first of five 'Last steam trains to Exeter' run that year! The turntable was removed later that year and the shed closed in March 1967. Visible on the left is the 'new' Exmouth Junction signal box, built a little to the west of the original in 1959.

A revival of sorts occurred on 8 April 1995 when Nos 75014 and 70000 *Britannia* were serviced after arriving on an 0800 Preston to Exeter St David's rail tour. They are standing on a road retained to access the wagon repair shops. *R. A. Lumber/DHM*

EXMOUTH JUNCTION: When the Exmouth line opened, a double-track junction was provided, but the branch was single and it was not until 1908 that it was doubled to Topsham. The original 1875 signal box is pictured at 3.35pm on 23 May 1952 as 'E1/R' Class No 32697 leaves the yard with a down transfer freight. The engine shed can just be seen above the train, with the tall water tank and coaling-plant particularly prominent. On the left 'Z' Class 0-8-0T No 30954 is shunting in the marshalling yard, its regular duty. To its left are the Carriage & Wagon shops.

The LSWR box was replaced by a brick-built 64-lever structure in November 1959. The lever frame was removed in January 1988 and a panel installed; the box now operates as a 'fringe' to the Exeter Signalling Centre at St David's. On 25 February 1998 DMU No 150219 is joining the down main with the 1024 Exmouth to Barnstaple service. On the left Nos 37156 and 37711 are reversing the second portion of their stone train into the yard. *Derek Frost/DHM*

EXMOUTH JUNCTION FREIGHT YARD was a sorting yard of ten sidings, which in 1951 was handling up to 700 wagons daily. No facilities were provided for handling freight – all local traffic was dealt with at Exeter Central. On 11 December 1951 0-6-2T No 32695 is shunting at the throat of the yard. The building in the left background is the concrete works, which opened in 1913.

The works closed in 1963 and a coal concentration depot was opened on its site in 1967, four of the sidings being removed at this time. Coal traffic ceased in 1991 and thereafter the yard was used only occasionally for permanent way traffic. However, in 1998 a terminal was established to receive stone dust for a fibre-optic-cable-laying contract. Thirty-eight trains ran until 2000, but ceased when the contractors went into liquidation. Nos 37156/711 are seen again after arrival with the first portion of their train from Whatley Quarry. The 18-wagon load had to be split in Riverside Yard as it was too heavy for the climb from St David's to Central stations. *Derek Frost/DHM*

MOUNT PLEASANT HALT was another of the 1906 halts, opening on 26 January immediately to the east of the 262-yard-long Blackboy Tunnel. No waiting shelters were provided and access to the platforms was via two steep paths – needless to say, traffic was light! The path to the up platform can be noted above 'T9' 4-4-0 No 716 as it passes the halt in about 1924 with a Waterloo train. The 'Greyhound' is in original condition, and was rebuilt with a superheater and extended smokebox in 1927. The west end of Exmouth Junction marshalling yard is on the right.

The halt closed on 2 January 1928, and there is nothing to hint of its existence in May 1951, but for the path that provides railway staff with easy access to the yard. 'Battle of Britain' 4-6-2 No 34061 *73 Squadron* is storming out of the tunnel with the 2.30pm Exeter Central to Waterloo train.

The top of the cutting still provides a fine view on Sunday 2 August 1981 as 'Hoover' No 50002 *Superb* powers the 1225 Exeter St David's to Waterloo service. In addition to the expected coal wagons on the far right, the yard also contains a rake of clay wagons awaiting attention at the Exmouth Junction wagon repair shops. The loco was refurbished at Doncaster Works in 1983.

The cutting is now typically overgrown, but a gap in the trees and bushes allows this 8 June 2005 view of a fourth generation of power over this route, Nos 159021/018 forming the 1010 Exeter St David's to Waterloo service. *R. A. Lumber collection/R. A. Lumber/DHM(2)*

ST JAMES'S PARK HALT was the third of the 1906 halts, opening as Lions Holt Halt, also on 26 January. The name was changed on 7 October 1946, the new one referring to the adjacent Exeter City Football Club ground. This stop was provided with a basic shelter on the up platform. Drummond '700' Class 3F 0-6-0 No 30691 passes with a freight for Exmouth Junction on 3 October 1959.

The only one of the halts to survive today; about two-thirds of weekday Exmouth branch services stop here. Currently all Sunday trains call, such as No 150266 forming the 1014 Exeter St David's to Exmouth service on 8 May 2005. *R. A. Lumber/DHM*

ST JAMES'S PARK HALT: The down platform is longer than the up one, and 'Schools' Class 5P 4-4-0 No 30913 *Christ's Hospital* passes it with the 3.05pm Waterloo to Exeter Central train on 12 September 1959. Some of this class worked on this route in their later days after electrification displaced them from their native South East. Visible at the top of the picture is the football club's 1926-built grandstand.

Although the ground has been largely modernised in recent years, the timber-built grandstand still looks down on Nos 153318 and 150251 as they pass with the 1124 Exmouth to Exeter St David's service on 5 January 2005. Up the Grecians! *R. A. Lumber/DHM*

EXETER CENTRAL: 'Battle of Britain' 4-6-2 No 34076 *41 Squadron* approaches the Howell Road bridge as it arrives with the 11.30am Brighton to Plymouth train on 8 October 1964. It is 25 minutes late, presumably due to the failure of the rostered diesel. On the right are two carriage sidings, while on the extreme left is a road leading to the goods yard. The semaphores on the fine gantry, from left to right, route to the down through, the down main (Platform 2) and a bay (Platform 1).

On 5 September 2004 another Bulleid 'Pacific' (No 34027 *Taw Valley*, masquerading as No 34045 *Ottery St Mary*) approaches through the 'jungle' with a 'Cathedrals Express' charter. In another identity crisis, it is carrying an 'Atlantic Coast Express' headboard – all very confusing! The sidings have been lifted and a relay room built. Overgrown rails still lead towards the site of the goods yard but have been disconnected from the main line. *R. A. Lumber/DHM*

EXETER CENTRAL: Looking in the opposite direction from the same bridge, we see what is perhaps the classic view of this station. The layout is the result of an almost total rebuild that was completed in 1933, with official re-opening on 1 July that year. Previously Exeter Queen Street, the station was also renamed to go with its new image, and two new signal boxes were opened to replace three earlier structures. The 'new' 'A' box is pictured at 12.55pm on 2 August 1953, as 'H15' 4-6-0 No 30482 departs with what appears to be a special comprising ex-LMS stock.

The signal box closed on 6 May 1985 when its remaining operations were taken over by a new panel at Exeter St David's. The building remained in use by the permanent way department for several years, but extensive damage caused by burst water pipes led to its demolition. On 15 March 2003 Class 52 No D1015 *Western Champion* passes through the basic layout with the 1336 Okehampton to Crewe, the returning 'Western Quarryman' tour. *J. H. Bamsey/DHM*

EXETER CENTRAL: We are now looking from New North Road back towards the bridge from which the previous pictures were taken, and can now appreciate the additional length of the up platform; the down one does not start until immediately below us. The cattle dock is on the left and a DMU sits in the carriage shed, which was erected in 1930 on a site once occupied by the original engine shed. Ivatt 2-6-2T No 41216 is on the down through road with a transfer freight to Riverside Yard at 15.13 on 13 April 1965.

The up through road was taken out of use in November 1969 and the same fate befell the down through road in October 1984. The carriage sidings were taken out of use in 1970 and the area now forms part of a car park. No 159007 is departing with the 1240 Paignton to Waterloo service on 8 October 2002. *R. A. Lumber/DHM*

EXETER CENTRAL: The original Queen Street station was built in the Longbrook Valley, itself originally part of the moat of the nearby Norman Rougemont Castle. It was relatively small with an overall roof, and was a dark and smoky place. In contrast the rebuilt facility was spacious and airy and more in keeping with its status. However, it is pictured here on a day that would mark a serious downturn in its fortunes – the last scheduled full day of regular steam working, 5 September 1964. No 34056 *Croydon* is arriving in Platform 2 with the 11.45 Waterloo to Ilfracombe service, which will be taken forward by No 34084 *253 Squadron*. On the left No 34107 *Blandford Forum* is on an up troop special, and is moving up over the scissors crossover to take water. Overlooking it is Exeter Prison; it must be particularly galling for the inmates watching all those trains offering a potential trip to freedom!

In the 'present' view No 150230 departs forming the 1154 Barnstaple to Exmouth service on 30 May 2005. *R. A. Lumber/DHM*

EXETER CENTRAL: The castle is up on the hillside to the right of No 34057 *Biggin Hill*, which is arriving with the 10.35 Waterloo to Padstow on 1 August 1964, which will be taken forward by 'N' Class No 31859. In the foreground is the scissors crossover, used for combining different portions of up trains: a typical scenario would have the first portion stopping before the scissors and the loco detached and run over them to Exmouth Junction. The engine for Waterloo would be standing further up the platform, and would then back on to the train and draw it forward to the end of the platform. Next, another loco would propel restaurant cars over the scissors and on to the front portion. Finally, a second train would arrive and, after its engine had departed, the main portion would reverse onto it.

The station is now a pale shadow of itself and locomotive-hauled trains are rare. However, on 13 April 2005 Royal engine No 67005 *Queen's Messenger* is heading the track-recording train. *R. A. Lumber/DHM*

EXETER CENTRAL: The main goods yard and shed were located to the north of the station, with a smaller yard at the west end and a coal wharf near the carriage shed. In the 1950s up to four daily transfer trips were made in each direction, to and from Exmouth Junction yard. A Fyffes banana depot was established in the goods yard, supplied by special trains from Southampton Docks. However, the goods yard closed to general traffic in December 1967; a Blue Circle cement terminal had been established there, however, and trains from Westbury cement works continued to run. On 17 July 1984 No 47246 has arrived with the 7B22 MTTHO 1610 from Westbury and is shunting the vacuum-braked Presflo wagons into position.

The terminal closed in January 1990, No 08953 clearing the final empty wagons from the yard on the 19th of that month. During June 2005 a block of apartments was nearing completion. *Both DHM*

Lyme Regis branch

COMBPYNE: The Axminster & Lyme Regis Light Railway opened on 24 August 1903. Although independent, the LSWR had a financial interest in the company, and gained control of it in 1907 when it ran into financial difficulties. The only intermediate station on the branch was situated here, about three-quarters of a mile from its namesake village. On 16 August 1959 Adams 4-4-2T No 30582 is approaching with the 3.57pm Lyme Regis to Axminster train. It is passing a siding that was converted from a crossing loop in 1930, a signal box closing at the same time. The sharp curvature of the track and low axle limit restricted the types of engines that could be used on the branch, and the veteran Adams 'Radial' tanks were the mainstay from 1913 to 1961.

Today the station building is occupied as a house, and the minor road bridge in the background still fulfils its purpose. It is, however, obscured by trees in May 2005. *Terry Gough/DHM*

CANNINGTON VIADUCT: This substantial concrete ten-arch structure was the main engineering feature on the line, and was an early example built by 'Concrete Bob' McAlpine. Soon after completion the first pier and west abutment settled vertically due to the sandy foundations not accepting the load, and a jack arch was constructed in the third arch to stop any further settlement. This feature stands out on 13 August 1960 as 'Radials' Nos 30582 and 30584 pass over with the 10.45am Waterloo to Lyme Regis train.

The branch closed from 29 November 1965, but the viaduct is listed and still spans this peaceful valley in May 2005. (The branch terminus is just over the county boundary in Dorset, and is thus featured in *BR Past & Present* Nos 29 and 44.) *Terry Gough/DHM*

Seaton branch

COLYTON: The Seaton & Beer Railway opened on 16 March 1868, and although it was an independent company it was leased to the LSWR from the outset. Colyton station was built on high ground on the east side of the River Coly, the village being situated on the opposite bank. The 'M7' 0-4-4Ts worked the branch for many years until 1963. On 8 August 1960 No 30048 is departing past the goods yard by propelling the 7.05pm Seaton Junction to Seaton push-pull train.

The station re-opened on 8 March 1980 as the new northern terminus of the Seaton & District Tramway. On 7 June 2005 Car No 7 is departing with the 1510 Colyton to Seaton service. This tram was built in 1958 and is based on an ex-Bournemouth open-topper used on the Llandudno & Colwyn Bay system. *Terry Gough/DHM*

COLYFORD: The other intermediate station on this 4½-mile branch was a simple affair comprising a single platform with no sidings. 'M7' No 30045 is about to depart and pass over a level crossing with the 3.52pm Seaton to Seaton Junction train on 5 August 1962.

The 2ft 9in gauge tramway commenced operations near Seaton in 1970, and extended to Colyford on 9 April 1971. Tram car No 16 is approaching the A3052 crossing with the 1120 Seaton to Colyton service on 9 May 2005. The flashing lights and lifting barriers have been set in operation by the driver before departure. Originally Bournemouth car 106 and dating from 1921, this tram was rebuilt at Seaton between 1974 and 1991. *R. A. Lumber/DHM*

SEATON: From south of Colyford, the branch ran alongside the picturesque Axe estuary to the terminus. The original station was completely rebuilt in 1935-36 when a long island platform was provided. Looking across the Axe on 28 July 1957 five through coaches sit in Platform 1 with the branch train in No 2. The engine shed and water tank are visible on the left.

The branch closed on 7 March 1966, and the May 2005 view shows a large building standing on the station site; this was an electronics factory, which is itself now closed. The tramway's depot and works are just out of sight on the right, from where the tramway leaves the old branch formation to follow a different route into town. *Terry Gough/DHM*

Sidmouth branch

NEAR SIDMOUTH JUNCTION: On Saturday 27 June 1964 Ivatt 2MT 2-6-2T No 41295 curves away down the branch at 1.16pm with the 9.00am Waterloo to Exmouth and Sidmouth train; this arrived behind No 34088 *213 Squadron*, and comprises three coaches for Sidmouth and eight for Exmouth. The DMU in the background is in the sidings seen on page 22. Branch services had been dieselised in the previous year, but steam continued to deputise occasionally, as well as hauling the summer Saturday through trains in 1964.

The branch formation survives but is heavily overgrown on 2 April 2005. The rear of the 1020 Waterloo to Exeter Class 159 can be glimpsed on the main line as it slows for its Feniton stop. *Derek Frost/DHM*

NEAR SIDMOUTH JUNCTION: The previous photos were taken from a minor road bridge, and this is in view as Standard 4MT 2-6-4T No 80059 heads for Tipton St John's with an empty stock working at 11.24am on 27 June 1964.

Since closure, the cutting has been filled in and the land now forms part of a large orchard. Standing on the same spot the view is obscured by trees, and a position to the left was chosen for the April 2005 comparison. Although modern fencing has been erected on the left, original concrete posts survive from the railway boundary fence. *Derek Frost/DHM*

NEAR SIDMOUTH JUNCTION: The branch continued in a cutting, and about three-quarters of a mile from the junction passed under the main A30 trunk road near Fenny Bridges, before following the valley of the River Otter to the south. Recorded from the road bridge, No 80039 is heading the 8.33am Sidmouth Junction to Sidmouth train on 19 August 1963.

Although now part of a field, the lighter area in the April 2005 photo represents the infilled cutting. From 1997 an even more dramatic transformation took place when work started on the new A30 dual carriageway from Honiton to Exeter. The original piece of road remains open, with the bridge in situ. A 4WD can be seen in place of the 4MT – a rather poor substitute! *R. A. Lumber/DHM*

OTTERY ST MARY: The 8¼-long Sidmouth Railway opened on 6 July 1874, operated as a branch of the LSWR, despite being built by an independent company. The first of the two intermediate stations was situated in the Otter Valley, to the west of the town centre, and is seen here on 4 March 1967, the last day of passenger services. The Sidmouth-bound DMU is departing at 1648 past the 1955-built signal box, and over a level crossing.

On 30 April 2005 the main building survives as 'The Station Youth Centre', while to its north an industrial estate covers the formation, with a building immediately behind the camera. *R. A. Lumber/DHM*

TIPTON ST JOHN'S: Originally a passing point on the Sidmouth branch, the station became a junction in May 1897 when the line to Budleigh Salterton opened. A new 33-lever signal box was commissioned at that time, and is pictured here from the level crossing immediately south of the station on 21 September 1963 as No 80067 departs at 4.06pm with a Sidmouth Junction to Sidmouth train. The loco will soon be climbing out of the Otter Valley at a gradient of 1 in 45. The footbridge had been covered, but lost its roof in the 1950s.

The main station building is now a dwelling, and can just be seen on the left above the hedge on 7 May 2005. More prominent is a surviving crossing gate post. *R. A. Lumber/DHM*

SIDMOUTH: Pannier tank No 4666 approaches the island platform with the LCGB 'East Devon Railtour' at 1350 on 28 February 1965 – a rare steam working at that date, but one that was to be repeated with a re-run of the tour one week later. The 23-lever signal box is on the right.

The box survived until the passenger service to this genteel resort ended on 4 March 1967, although coal traffic lasted a further two months. The site of the station is now occupied by several businesses with the main building and goods shed still standing. This particular area is now the headquarters for a construction company, as recorded on 9 May 2005. *R. A. Lumber/DHM*

Routes to Exmouth

NEWTON POPPLEFORD: Two passengers await the arrival of Ivatt tank No 41308 and the 1.14pm train from Tipton St John's to Exmouth on 9 August 1960. The station had opened on 1 June 1899, more than two years after services on the Budleigh Salterton Railway commenced. The single siding on the left provided accommodation for camping coaches for many years.

The site is undeveloped in May 2005, and the gateway and house on the left are the best reference points when comparing the two views. The latter's chimneys can be seen above the goods van in the 'past' view. *Terry Gough/DHM*

EAST BUDLEIGH: A little later on the same day, No 41308 is returning from Exmouth with the 1.28pm to Tipton St John's. A concrete-built feed store can be seen in the goods yard on the left. The station opened with the line, close to the village of Otterton, East Budleigh being a mile to the west.

After closure the main station building was converted to an attractive dwelling. This is, however, largely obscured by trees in June 2005. The former feed store also survives today. The current boundary fence is a few feet closer to the house than the previous railway one. *Terry Gough/DHM*

BUDLEIGH SALTERTON: The station serving this seaside town was a terminus from 1897 until 1 June 1903, when the LSWR completed an extension to Exmouth. Standard Prairie tank No 82024 stands with the 3.20pm train to Exmouth on 9 August 1960; it has just run round its two coaches after arriving with the 2.50pm from Exmouth. The goods yard is behind the camera.

The final trains over this line ran on 4 March 1967 and housing now covers the station area. The exact position of the 'past' photograph is within the building on the left, but the road overbridge still stands, albeit hidden by the trees beyond the far dwelling. For many years a supermarket occupied the goods yard land, but that too has now been developed for housing. *Terry Gough/DHM*

LITTLEHAM was the only intermediate station on the extension, built on a curve adjacent to the village. The station building possessed an ornate canopy, clearly visible as the 1605 Exmouth to Tipton St John's DMU calls on 18 February 1967. It is raining, and the dismal day is perhaps appropriate as the line has another only two weeks to live. The signal box is to the right of the camera, and beyond that is the goods yard, which was also used to berth stock, such as that used on the Exmouth to Cleethorpes service (see page 10).

The station building is now a dwelling, as recorded on 5 May 2005, with other housing built around it. *R. A. Lumber/DHM*

EXMOUTH: Brunel originally proposed building a broad gauge branch from Exminster to Exmouth via a bridge spanning the River Exe to Topsham. The impending arrival of the LSWR heralded a change in plans, and instead a 9½-mile-long standard gauge branch from Exmouth Junction opened on 1 May 1861, less than a year after the LSWR had reached Exeter. That company worked the line from the outset and absorbed it ten years later. The original station had an island platform, but was rebuilt in 1924 when two such platforms were provided. Photographed from Platform 3 on 12 August 1960, No 82025 is departing from No 2 with the 11.45am train to Exeter Central.

The latter is the only platform to survive today, albeit shortened at the southern end. Trees and bushes are now growing beside the boundary fence, but a gap allowed this view on 7 June 2005. *Terry Gough/DHM*

EXMOUTH: The original timber-built engine shed was replaced by a 70-foot-long single-road concrete building in 1927. It was a sub-shed to Exmouth Junction and normally had an allocation of four tank engines. Class 'O2' 0-4-4T No 30232 is 'on shed' on Sunday 2 September 1951. This class was largely supplanted by Standard 2-6-2Ts in the following year.

DMUs took over most services in September 1963 and the shed closed in November that year. Platform 4, the one retained in 1968 when the station was 'rationalised', is to the right of the camera; however, this was replaced by the original Platform 2 in 1976, and the subsequent building of a new relief road involved the demolition of much of the station. The May 2005 view was taken from an embankment that runs through the shed site with the road to the immediate right. The houses on the left are the link between the pictures. *R. A. Lumber/DHM*

EXMOUTH: The west side of the station on 21 June 1949 finds 1939-built Devon General AEC Regal No XR 420 parked next to the cattle dock. Behind it, a push-pull fitted 'M7' tank has arrived in Platform 1. To the left of the photographer is a sizeable goods yard built on land reclaimed from the sea in the 1920s. Behind the goods shed a short branch ran down to the nearby docks.

Traffic to the docks ended in 1967, the goods yard closed at the same time, and much of the latter is now used for car parking. In 1975 work started on a new transport interchange, which opened on 2 May 1976 when the re-instated former Platform 2 came into use. The combined bus and rail stations are pictured in May 2005. *J. H. Bamsey/DHM*

EXMOUTH: Steam days are drawing to a close as ex-GWR 0-6-0PT No 3759 departs for Exmouth Junction yard with the daily freight at 3.14pm on 7 November 1964. It has just joined the main running line after leaving the yard on the right. The branch to Tipton St John's can be noted curving away in front of the houses to the left and starting its 1 in 50 climb to Littleham, and the roof of the 70-lever signal box is just visible above the brake-van. One steam passenger duty survived on the branch until January 1965, subsequently leaving the freight to be steam-hauled until 24 May of that year.

Today this location is within a marine engineering yard and the view of the railway is obscured. A position a little to the south was selected on 5 May 2005 to witness No 150253 departing as the 1554 service to Paignton. Much of the former goods yard to the right is now used for parking. *R. A. Lumber/DHM*

LYMPSTONE: From the Exmouth direction, the branch crosses the heart of the village on a short embankment before entering the station. Standard 2-6-2T No 82011 is departing with an Exmouth to Exeter Central service in August 1953. The train is hiding a goods loop/siding, and the signal box is located on the single platform, next to the station building.

The goods yard and signal box were closed in 1960 and 1962 respectively, and the station buildings were demolished in 1976, with a basic shelter now provided; the station was renamed Lympstone Village in May 1991. No 150233 is departing with the 1724 Exmouth to Barnstaple service on 5 May 2005. *R. A. Lumber/DHM*

LYMPSTONE: The railway now runs beside the shore of the Exe estuary for more than 2 miles, providing superb views of an area that is a noted bird habitat. On 5 September 1963 No 82001 approaches Lympstone with the 5.15pm Exeter Central to Tipton St John's train.

The avocet is a wading bird that winters here and has given its name to the branch, which is marketed today as 'The Avocet Line'. Two single units, Nos 153329 and 153302, combine to form the 1319 Paignton to Exmouth service on 5 May 2005. The high-rise buildings in the background are part of the Royal Marines Commando Training Centre. *Derek Frost/DHM*

EXTON: The railway bridges a small watercourse immediately south of the station. In October 1960 severe flooding weakened the bridge and in the following year it was replaced by a redundant structure from Lapford. On a more temperate day, 26 August 1963, No 80040 is about to cross the replacement with the 6.23pm Exmouth to Exeter Central train.

No 153380 forms the 1624 Exmouth to Paignton service on 30 May 2005, half a mile after passing Lympstone Commando, a station that opened in May 1976 for the exclusive use of staff and marines at the training centre – disembarkation here is not recommended as you will be greeted by armed guards! *Derek Frost/DHM*

EXTON station, located beside the estuary, was originally named Woodbury Road, referring to a village some 2 miles away, but was renamed after its adjacent village in September 1958. Ivatt No 41306 pauses at its single platform with an Exmouth to Exeter Central train at 7.1pm on 5 September 1963.

The station is now a request stop, with more than half of the branch services eligible to call. On 30 May 2005 No 150265 has stopped to collect two passengers and is departing as the 1554 Exmouth to Paignton service. The station house is now a private dwelling with a chalet bungalow erected beside it. *Derek Frost/DHM*

TOPSHAM: On Thursday 7 August 1958 No 82019 has arrived with the 1.25pm from Exeter Central, and has run around its stock before forming the 1.45pm return working. The goods yard, complete with its sizeable shed, is on the right. Behind the photographer a 700-yard-long branch had run down to the quay, but this had closed in the previous year. Both quay and branch had been built by the LSWR and opened on 23 September 186, with facilities primarily intended to transfer goods bound for Exeter from ships that were too large for the city's canal.

Today the station is the only passing point on the branch and is used regularly for this purpose when the basic half-hourly service is operating. On 5 May 2005 No 150233 is departing as the 1350 Exeter St David's to Exmouth service, while No 150249 heads into the distance with the 1354 Exmouth to Paignton service. A road now follows the route of the quay branch. *R. A. Lumber/DHM*

TOPSHAM: Pictured from the level crossing, which is used by the main road to Exmouth, at 15.50 on 28 February 1965, Nos 4666 and 41206 double-head the LCGB special seen previously at Sidmouth. The Gothic-styled main building is another example of the work of Sir William Tite.

The crossing gates were replaced by full lifting barriers in 1973, and the signal box closed in January 1988 when colour light signals came into use, controlled from Exmouth Junction. The box was occupied as an office for a period, but is currently disused. The main building has lost its canopy but also survives in private use. No 150219 departs with the 0924 Exmouth to Exeter St David's service on 7 June 2005. *R. A. Lumber/DHM*

DIGBY & SOWTON: On Tuesday 7 April 1964 Standard 2-6-4T No 80037 is approaching the Apple Lane bridge with the 5.49pm Exeter Central to Exmouth train. The large Digby Hospital, founded in 1886 as the Exeter City Asylum, is close by and the train will soon pass the site of a siding that had been used until 1957 to deliver coal there. The branch was single track throughout when opened, but increasing traffic led to the doubling of the Exmouth Junction to Topsham section in May 1908.

The line was singled again in February 1973 and today the cutting sides are typically overgrown. Another change is the appearance of a footbridge, which belongs to Digby & Sowton Halt, opened on 23 May 1995 to serve an industrial estate, business parks and housing, including the re-developed hospital site. No 150219 is leaving the halt's single platform with the 1350 Exeter St David's to Exmouth service on 17 May 2005. *Derek Frost/DHM*

DIGBY & SOWTON: Ivatt 2-6-2T No 41323 is hauling the 6.20pm Exeter Central to Exmouth train on 9 July 1963. The rear of the train has just passed the site of Clyst St Mary & Digby Halt, which was situated on the far side of a road bridge. The halt was open from May 1908 to September 1948, the first part of its name referring to a village almost a mile to the east.

Rather than take the 'present' photo from within the trees, a telephoto lens shot from Digby & Sowton's footbridge shows track relaying taking place on an overcast and damp 22 March 2005. The approximate position of No 41323 is to the right of the nearest digger. No 66043 is on the ballast train, and is standing at the site of the original halt. *R. A. Lumber/DHM*

HILL BARTON: On Sunday 4 April 1957 another 'Ivatt', No 41306, climbs with the 3.00pm train from Exeter Central to Exmouth towards a bridge that carries Exeter's bypass over the branch.

A second ballast train on 22 March 2005 finds Nos 66060 and 66063 top-and-tailing the 1225 train from Westbury to Exmouth Junction, where the engineering possession commenced. While once such work was largely undertaken overnight, Network Rail prefers the efficiencies and cost savings gained by longer closures, even if this inconveniences the travelling public. On this occasion the branch was closed for a whole week while track was relayed, with a substitute bus service in operation. *R. A. Lumber/DHM*

POLSLOE BRIDGE HALT opened on 31 May 1908 (together with Clyst St Mary & Digby), when the doubled section of line came into use, and a steam railmotor service commenced between Exeter and Topsham. The platforms were rebuilt and extended in 1927 using components from the nearby concrete works. No 80039 is arriving with the 12.55pm Exeter Central to Topsham service on 14 June 1963. Exmouth Junction's massive concrete mechanical coaling-plant can be seen to the right of the engine; this station was a popular destination for loco spotters wanting to 'bash' the shed!

The trio of 22 March 2005 pictures is completed by Nos 66043 and 66033 top-and-tailing the 1132 Westbury to Exmouth Junction ballast working. *R. A. Lumber/DHM*

Exeter St David's to Whiteball

EXETER ST DAVID'S: When the LSWR extended its route from Exeter Queen Street to the Bristol & Exeter's station at St David's on 1 February 1862, the connection was made down a gradient of 1 in 37, which meant that most up trains required the assistance of one or more banking engines. For a number of years Exmouth Junction had an allocation of four Stroudley 'E1/R' 0-6-2Ts for banking and transfer goods duties. This era is drawing to a close, however, at 7.45pm on 23 May 1959 as No 32697 banks an up freight; it is the last of the class operating locally and will shortly be replaced by 'Z' Class 0-8-0Ts.

On 25 June 2005 'Hastings' DEMU No 1001 arrives with the 0643 ex-Hastings 'West Country Cruiser' charter. *R. A. Lumber/DHM*

EXETER ST DAVID'S station opened on 1 May 1844 when the broad gauge Bristol & Exeter Railway reached its destination. It was subsequently rebuilt in both 1862-4 and 1911-4, to enable it to cope with Devon's developing railway network. As part of the latter work, a bay platform was provided at the northern end of the station, with a parcels platform known as Hyde Park adjacent to it. 'Bulldog' Class 4-4-0 No 3341 *Blasius* is in this siding on a snowy 20 January 1949 while on station pilot duty.

The middle siding here was removed as part of the 1985 re-signalling. Hyde Park is now normally used for stabling DMUs, but on 21 November 2004 No 57605 *Totnes Castle* is a rare occupant. The former No 47206, re-engined with a General Motors power unit, it had been sent from Plymouth Laira the previous day to rescue an ailing HST. In the event it was not needed and is now awaiting a driver to return it to Laira. *J. H. Bamsey/DHM*

EXETER ST DAVID'S: The bay platform (No 2) was the usual home for Exe Valley line services. On Saturday 21 September 1963 Collett 0-4-2T No 1450 is departing with the 10.25am service to Dulverton, two weeks before services over this route were withdrawn. A diesel shunter is sitting in Hyde Park.

On 22 April 2005 Freightliner's No 47150 is arriving to pick up a train crew before heading to Meldon Quarry on a route-learning trip. *R. A. Lumber/DHM*

EXETER ST DAVID'S: When the LSWR reached agreement with the B&E for its trains to run through the station over the latter's metals, it was required to stop all its trains here. A novel feature of their different approaches to the station also meant that up Paddington and Waterloo workings travelled in opposite directions. Platform 4 was normally used by down LSWR (and later Southern) trains. However, on 1 October 1960 we have the unusual sight of 4MT 2-6-2T No 4167 leaving on an up Paddington train. The Western's main line is flooded at Hele & Bradninch and the train is being sent via the Exe Valley line.

Since the opening of Exeter's MAS power box in May 1985, Platform 4 is now the down main for services to the West. On 11 June 2005 the 1405 Paddington to Plymouth HST (with power cars Nos 43040/018) is arriving as DMU No 159009 heads from Platform 3 to New Yard after terminating with the 1601 service from Honiton. *R. A. Lumber/DHM*

EXETER ST DAVID'S: At one time the GWR operated five signal boxes in the vicinity of the station. West box can be seen on page 80, while here Middle box is prominent as Standard 2-10-0 No 92203 arrives in Platform 1 at 3.47pm with the 9.5am Swansea to Kingswear train on 1 August 1959; this was a regular 9F duty at that time. 'M7' No 30044 is in the spur used to hold banking engines. The 95-lever box had a narrow brick base due to its location in limited space between two tracks. It controlled the east end of the station as well as the Red Cow level crossing, which at this time passed over no fewer than 14 tracks, including goods lines to the left of the picture. Its unusual name is derived from the nearby inn and village. Visible just to the right of the box is the transfer shed, originally built to tranship goods between standard and broad gauge wagons.

The box closed on 30 March 1985 and was demolished soon afterwards. The 11 June 2005 scene includes Nos 159001/017 approaching Platform 1 from New Yard before forming the 1610 departure to Waterloo, and 'Voyager' No 221140 arriving with the 1025 Newcastle to Plymouth service. *Peter W. Gray/DHM*

EXETER GOODS YARD BOX: Situated at the west end of Red Cow crossing and separated from Middle box by nine tracks, this small structure opened in February 1896 and contained five levers, its main purpose being to protect the crossing. Two of the roads were through lines allowing goods trains to avoid St David's station. On 31 July 1971 Class 22 diesel-hydraulic No 6338 is arriving with the 0920 freight from Barnstaple.

The box closed from 26 February 1978 when the goods avoiding lines were closed and the track over the crossing severed. The scene on 8 May 2005 shows the road entrance to Riverside Yard. Several truncated and little-used sidings are out of view on the right, with DMU storage sidings to the left of the camera. *R. A. Lumber/DHM*

EXETER RIVERSIDE YARD opened on 25 October 1943 to handle the increased levels of traffic during the Second World War. It had two through lines and seven sidings; six more sidings were added in 1966 and a further two in 1978. A second-hand 54-lever signal box from Hatherley Junction, Cheltenham, was provided to control the goods lines and connections to the sidings. It is pictured on 9 October 1971 with the yard to its right and behind. D6334 is in New Yard on the opposite side of the main line, prior to working milk empties to Hemyock. East box is just out of sight to the left.

East box closed in 1973 and Riverside box suffered a similar fate in April 1981. Current use of the yard is minimal, but in an unusual burst of activity on 13 April 2005 No 66015 is arriving with the 0933 Burngullow to Irvine china clay slurry train. It will pick up additional tanks that have been already forwarded here, a full load being too heavy for the Royal Albert Bridge and South Devon banks. It is passing No 67025, which is laying over with a test train. *Both DHM*

COWLEY BRIDGE JUNCTION: The broad gauge Exeter & Crediton Railway opened on 12 May 1851. It was leased to the Bristol & Exeter and diverged from that line at this location, 1¼ miles north of St David's. From 1862 the lease was transferred to the LSWR, and eventually the line became part of the Southern Railway. On 21 May 1956 former GWR 2-6-0 No 6385 is signalled to take this route with the 11.46am Exeter Central to Plymouth. At this time it was a regular practice for Western and Southern loco crews to use their 'own' engines when maintaining route knowledge of both lines between Devon's principal cities, in case of diversions. On the right is Riverside's up departure line, with the down goods loop commencing on the left.

Both vegetation growth and the erection of housing means that the 20 April 2005 photo was taken a little further to the east. No 66184 is leaving Riverside with the 6S55 Burngullow to Irvine tanks. *J. H. Bamsey/DHM*

COWLEY BRIDGE JUNCTION: The original signal box was replaced in about 1894 by a new structure, housing a 16-lever frame to control the double-line junction. With the opening of Riverside Yard, the building was extended northwards in 1943 to enable it to house 44 levers. Probably one of the most photographed signal boxes in the country, it is passed by 'Hall' Class 5MT 4-6-0 No 4920 *Dumbleton Hall* with the 10.6am Cardiff to Plymouth train on Tuesday 12 March 1963.

Following the rebuilding of three nearby bridges on the former SR route, the line was singled across them and over the junction in November 1965, and the box was closed on 30 March 1985 under the Exeter MAS scheme. Freightliner's No 47197 passes the junction on 3 November 2004 with HST stock forming the 5Z50 1205 Eastleigh to Plymouth Laira transfer move. *Derek Frost/DHM*

PYNES: From Exeter the railway follows the valley of the River Exe until just south of Stoke Canon. As a rough guide, heavy rainfall on Exmoor is reflected in this area about 12 hours later and the river can rise at up to a foot an hour. Thereafter the main line is in the Culm Valley until just beyond Cullompton, and when both rivers are in flood, water levels can rise by as much as 2 feet per hour. Accordingly there has been a history of disruption to rail services over the years. On Monday 18 March 1963, less than half a mile east of Cowley Bridge Junction, the fields are partly flooded as 4-6-0 No 4991 *Cobham Hall* hauls the 11.00am Plymouth to Manchester in lieu of the diagrammed 'Warship'.

After major flooding in 2000, some relief work was completed including this channel and culvert. Nos 43150 and 43037 power the 0904 Penzance to Paddington HST on 17 May 2005. *Derek Frost/DHM*

STOKE CANON: The original station was a little further north and had staggered platforms on either side of a crossing. The crossing box was in use from 1876 to 1985 and stands today in a boarded-up state. It is the last one of B&E origin, and is listed. The new station opened on 1 July 1894 at the junction with the Exe Valley line, and was subsequently rebuilt when two through lines were provided in 1931. The village is half a mile away and, with a good bus service, the station was little used and became a relatively early casualty; closing from 13 June 1960. Almost a year later on 3 June it is passed at 11.49am by 'King' Class 4-6-0 No 6001 *King Edward VII* with a Paddington to Paignton train.

The building on the right survives in June 2005, occupied by an asphalt company as an office. The shadow in the right foreground is cast by the main station building, also occupied commercially. *R. A. Lumber/DHM*

STOKE CANON: 'Mogul' No 6319 approaches the station with a down freight on Saturday 18 February 1961. The Exe Valley line can be noted curving away to the left. The far side of the up island platform was used by most branch services and was signalled for reversible running. The track on the right forms part of the goods yard, which was served by a daily trip freight. Around this time there were two regular customers: a paper mill, which received coal and despatched paper, and an agricultural machinery dealer, who received tractors and the like.

On 29 May 2005 a grassy bank can just be noted following the Exe Valley formation. Housing has been built on part of the goods yard site. *R. A. Lumber/DHM*

REWE: Churchward 2-6-0 No 5311 is on the steady climb up the Culm Valley at 6.3pm on 27 May 1960 as it approaches Paddleford bridge with what is thought to be the 3.5pm Hackney Yard (Newton Abbot) to Rogerstone Class F freight, mainly comprising coal empties. In the background the village straddles the main Exeter to Tiverton road; the road bridge can just be discerned in the cutting.

  Currently this location is one of the few on this stretch of railway that is relatively clear, and is thus very popular with today's generation of railway photographers. On peak Saturdays in the summer of 2004, Virgin Trains operated some locomotive-hauled trains to cater for holiday traffic. On 7 August Nos 67003 and 67002 top-and-tail the 5A19 1800 Goodrington carriage sidings to Old Oak Common empty stock working. *Derek Frost/DHM*

REWE: Looking the other way from the previous pictures, at 5.42pm also on 27 May 1960, we see 'Grange' 4-6-0 No 6816 *Frankton Grange* heading the 3.5pm Bristol to Tavistock Junction Class D freight. Although partially hidden by the train, Rewe's six-lever signal box can be noted; it dated from 3 July 1934 and was one of four boxes in the Exeter area opened in summer months to shorten the block sections. In this case it was positioned about halfway between Stoke Canon and Silverton, each of those boxes being 2 miles away.

The box closed on 15 March 1964, and 'Police'-liveried No 47829 passes its site with the 0840 Glasgow to Penzance on 28 July 2002, less than two weeks before regular Virgin loco-hauled services ceased. *Derek Frost/DHM*

95

SILVERTON station was actually situated adjacent to the hamlet of Ellerhayes, its namesake town being more than 1½ miles away to the north-west. It had staggered platforms on either side of a road bridge, and the down one is pictured on 26 June 1966 as 'Merchant Navy' No 35023, formerly *Holland-Afrika Line*, passes with the Southern Counties Touring Society's Waterloo-Exeter-Westbury-Waterloo 'Devonshire Rambler' rail tour. The station had closed on 3 October 1964 and the waiting shelter previously sited in the foreground has been removed; an up refuge siding was also removed in September of that year.

On 3 June 2004 Mendip Rail's No 59005 *Kenneth J. Painter* passes with the 7C28 1114 Exeter to Westbury stone empties. Hanson currently operate an aggregate distribution terminal in Riverside Yard. *Peter W. Gray/DHM*

SILVERTON: Churchward 8F 2-8-0 No 3856 passes the up platform with a down freight at 11.55am on 9 December 1961. The exhaust is obscuring the original platform-mounted signal box, but its 30-lever 1928 replacement can be partially glimpsed next to the wagons in the small goods yard on the right. A half-mile private siding curved away from here to serve a paper mill, which produced paper from esparto grass imported from Spain; trainloads of grass would be stabled in the up refuge until the mill could accept them. BR engines were not allowed into the mill's siding so the wagons would be fly-shunted from the yard.

The goods yard closed in 1965 and now forms part of a farmyard. However, much of the mill siding was set in concrete and can be easily followed today. The 1012 Birmingham to Plymouth 'Voyager' passes on 29 May 2005. *R. A. Lumber/DHM*

HELE & BRADNINCH station opened with the line in 1844, and was located in the village of Hele, the suffix referring to a town on the hillside nearby. In this undated view from the up platform we can see the main building on the opposite side, with the signal box between it and the level crossing. This station also closed on 3 October 1964 when all local services were withdrawn between Exeter and Taunton.

The main building survives to this day. Looking back to 23 July 1983, Nos 43169 and 43170 are powering past with the 1245 Newcastle to Penzance cross-country HST service. *Lens of Sutton/DHM*

HELE & BRADNINCH signal box was open by 1874, and was extended in 1943 to accommodate the additional levers required to work new goods loops added as a wartime measure. Full lifting barriers replaced the crossing gates in 1970, and on 29 July 1972 Brush Type 4 No 1688 (later 47101) passes with an up relief train.

The box survived until 9 December 1985, controlling the goods loops and level crossing. It was then closed as part of the Exeter MAS scheme. Wessex Trains No 150247 passes over the crossing forming the 1643 Paignton to Cardiff Central service on 29 May 2005. Another 'break section' box had been located at Westcott (halfway between here and Cullompton) from 1934 to 1964, and had been supervised by Hele's Station Master. *Both DHM*

HELE & BRADNINCH: Yet another paper mill can be found here, and in 1919 a siding was laid into it from the goods yard. General goods facilities were withdrawn at this station in 1965, but coal continued to be brought in by rail to fire the mill. Also on 29 July 1972, 'Peak' No D137 (later 45014) is heading the 0955 Bradford Exchange to Paignton train, 'The Devonian'. The sidings on the left lead to the goods yard and mill and the line on the far right is the down goods loop.

Coal traffic ended in the early 1980s and only the main running lines survived the 1985 re-signalling. Nos 153303 and 158831 approach with an Arriva Trains Manchester to Penzance service on 29 May 2005. *Both DHM*

CULLOMPTON: This market town was another site for one of the original B&E stations. It was totally rebuilt in 1931 with two platform roads and two through lines provided to ease congestion. A new 49-lever signal box was also positioned on the up platform at this time, behind the camera in this undated view of the main buildings.

  The station was another victim of the October 1964 cull, and by peering over today's security fence any view is largely obscured by rampant growth. On 23 July 1983 it was still possible to gain access to the overgrown up platform and witness No 47501 on the 1A47 1455 St Austell to Paddington Motorail service. *Lens of Sutton/DHM*

CULLOMPTON: Photographed from a position next to the road bridge seen in the previous picture, No 50035 (a month after being named *Ark Royal*) is passing with the 1B66 1130 Paddington to Penzance 'Cornish Riviera' on 14 February 1978. Although the station buildings and footbridge have been demolished, the decaying platforms are still largely intact. Buildings remain in the goods yard on the right, including the large 1931 brick-built shed. Goods facilities had been withdrawn in May 1967.

The goods yard was used by a road transport company for several years and the buildings survived until a motorway service station was constructed in 1999, the M5 being just to the right of these views. Pioneer 'Shed' No 66001 stands with spoil wagons during an engineering possession on 8 May 2005. *Both DHM*

TIVERTON JUNCTION was another station that opened in 1844, when it was known as Tiverton Road, acting as a railhead for the Tiverton area. It was renamed when the Tiverton branch opened in 1848, and a bay platform was provided for that line. It was completely rebuilt in 1932 with four main tracks between two island platforms, the outer faces of which were used by Tiverton and Hemyock trains. On 15 September 1962 7F 2-8-0 No 4706 heads away from the station at 4.55pm with a down fitted freight. This was the exact type of duty for which Churchward designed this nine-strong class in 1919.

Photographed from the same farm occupation bridge, the 0640 Dundee to Plymouth 'Voyager' sprints westward on 9 June 2005. *Peter W. Gray/DHM*

TIVERTON JUNCTION: 'Castle' Class 4-6-0 No 7037 *Swindon* arrives in the up main platform with the 4.25pm Exeter St David's to Taunton stopper on Whit Monday 22 May 1961 – a menial task for an express engine, but one that reflects an era when diesel locos were rapidly appearing on the scene. Behind it is the large 120-lever signal box erected in 1932 to work the new layout, including an extensive down yard (to the left of the camera).

Tiverton Junction remained as the only intermediate station between Exeter and Taunton until closure on 9 May 1986, when it was replaced by Tiverton Parkway. Today this is a secure site and any access is difficult. However, a car dealer occupies part of the former goods yard, and by standing on an old dock it was possible to look over the fencing for this 8 June 2005 view of the Carmarthen to Penzance service operated by No 158820. The trees are growing on the remains of the down platform. The two sidings are occasionally used by engineering traffic, the one on the right being the truncated remains of the Hemyock branch platform track. *Derek Frost/DHM*

TIVERTON JUNCTION: Auto-fitted 0-4-2T No 1462 arrives with the 2.22pm from Tiverton, also on 22 May 1961. The single-road engine shed can be noted to the left of the auto-coach, while the buildings just visible beyond it belong to the Lloyd Maunder slaughterhouse, meat traffic providing revenue for the railway at this time.

The signal box closed on 3 March 1986 and was demolished in March 1990. Surprisingly the station buildings and footbridge survived for almost five years after closure, until demolition in April 1991. Two weeks later, on the 21st, this was a view from the up platform with sections of footbridge still to be taken off site. The approximate position of No 1462 is between these and the relay building. The two platform loops are still in use here and the location is now known as Tiverton Loops. *Derek Frost/DHM*

SAMPFORD PEVERELL HALT: A siding and signal box already existed here, but the station did not open until 9 July 1928, named after a village a mile to the west. It was rebuilt only four years later when the track was quadrupled, with platform loops. A new signal box was provided at this time and its roof is visible behind the train on 24 February 1963 as renowned 'A4' 4-6-2 No 60022 *Mallard* storms by with the LCGB's 'The West Countryman Rail Tour'.

The station was another October 1964 casualty and the loops and sidings were gradually taken out of use in the 1966-68 period. However, due to the site's convenient location adjacent to both the M5 motorway and A361 North Devon Link Road, the new Tiverton Parkway station opened here on 12 May 1986, replacing Tiverton Junction. An HST powered by Nos 43140 and 43195 calls with the 0855 Plymouth to Paddington service on 29 May 2005. *Derek Frost/DHM*

BURLESCOMBE: The railway runs through the village, with a road bridge straddling the station area. The platforms were to the east of this bridge (see the cover picture), but looking in the opposite direction, in an undated view, we see 4-6-0 No 5024 *Carew Castle* climbing with the up 'Cornishman'. Until 1961 a mile-long tramway curved away to the right, serving Westleigh Quarry. It was of 3-foot gauge when opened in 1875, but was 'standardised' in 1898 when it was connected to the goods loop visible in front of the signal box.

The box closed in July 1964, and housing was being erected on 29 May 2005 as Nos 43148 and 43034 passed with the 0950 Paignton to Paddington HST. *Author's collection/DHM*

EASTBROOK: 'Castle' Class No 5067 *St Fagans Castle* is climbing the 1 in 115 grade towards Whiteball Tunnel with the 10.5am Paignton to Paddington Whit Saturday 'extra', at 11.45am on 9 June 1962. It is approaching the 'black bridge', which carries a minor road from Burlescombe and is a favourite haunt of railway photographers. Westleigh Quarry can be seen on the hillside above the engine. On the left is the down relief line, almost three-quarters of a mile long, which was brought into use between Whiteball Siding signal box and Burlescombe in 1927.

The relief line was truncated in July 1964, leaving a loop for down freight trains, and the 'new' connection with the down main is seen on 24 July 1982 as English Electric Type 4 No 50037 *Illustrious* climbs with the 1045 Newquay to Paddington summer Saturday service.

The loop was removed when Whiteball Siding box closed. 'Voyager' No 221129 is working the 0930 Penzance to Glasgow service on 29 May 2005. *Peter W. Gray/DHM (2)*

EASTBROOK: Looking in the opposite direction on another summer Saturday, 1 July 1961, 'Castle' Class 4-6-0 No 4095 *Harlech* Castle is framed by Burlescombe's distant signals as it speeds downhill with the 7.30am Newcastle to Paignton at 4.36pm. Just visible beyond the rear of the train is the farm occupation bridge from which the photographs on pages 112 and 113 were taken.

The signals were subsequently replaced by those seen on page 109. On 24 July 1982 a typical Summer Saturday train of the period sees British Railways Sulzer-engined 'Peak' No 45062 taking another load of holidaymakers West on the 0924 Nottingham to Paignton train.

That rare event these days, a new freight service, sees No 60091 *An Teallach* hauling only the third working of the 0826 Cardiff Tidal Yard to Tavistock Junction scrap empties on 16 April 2003. The train will be loaded on Plymouth's Cattewater branch. *Peter W. Gray/DHM (2)*

WHITEBALL TUNNEL: The arrival of the B&E in Devon was delayed by a year due to the need to bore a 1,088-yard-long tunnel under the Blackdown Hills. During this period a temporary station at Beam Bridge, just west of Wellington, was the limit of operations. At 10.37am on 1 July 1961 4-6-0 No 6938 *Corndean Hall* is passing Whiteball Siding signal box with the 8.10am Newport to Paignton service. On the left is a spur to hold any banking engines that may have assisted a train on the climb of Wellington bank at up to 1 in 80. The box is a replacement, the original B&E building having burned down in 1955.

The spur was taken out of use in 1972 and the box closed on 3 March 1986. Only the tunnel mouth today proves that this is indeed the same place as the 0900 Glasgow to Penzance 'Voyager' passes on 9 June 2005. *Peter W. Gray/DHM*

WHITEBALL TUNNEL marks the county boundary between Somerset and Devon, and the signal box was at the summit of Wellington bank, almost 400 feet above sea level. A magnificent wooden bracket signal stood just out of sight to the right of the 'past' picture opposite, but by 16 July 1983 it had been replaced by a tubular steel one positioned nearer the tunnel. No 50011 *Centurion* is passing with the 0920 service from Liverpool to Penzance.

The siding on the right was kept for departmental use after closure of the box, but has since been removed. The 1545 Paddington to Penzance HST is pictured on 9 June 2005. *Both DHM*

Culm Valley Light Railway

COLDHARBOUR HALT: This was a pioneering light railway, promoted independently by local people but operated by the Great Western from its opening on 29 May 1876. Financial difficulties soon led to the GWR acquiring it in 1880. A siding had been laid here at Coldharbour in 1877, mainly to serve the adjacent woollen mill; a steam engine was installed to supplement the water wheel, and coal became a major traffic. The halt opened in February 1929, and the mill is seen on the right as No 1450 arrives with the 5.10pm train from Tiverton Junction to Hemyock on 3 September 1963, during the last week of passenger services.

The mill now operates as a museum with a car park on the site of the halt. Guided tours operate, with textile machine demonstrations. Behind the camera a footpath follows the formation to Uffculme village centre. *Derek Frost/DHM*

UFFCULME: 0-4-2T No 1421 arrives at one of the original stations on 13 October 1962 with the 1.45pm Tiverton Junction to Hemyock train. On the left, beyond the crossing gates, is an animal feed mill that provided traffic for the railway. In the foreground is the loop siding that had once passed through a small timber goods shed. Track curvature and low axle limits restricted the stock that could be used on this line. The coach is one of two ex-Barry Railway vehicles that replaced elderly GWR stock in 1950; dating from 1920, they were rebuilt at Swindon with gas lighting, as slow speeds on the branch were insufficient to keep carriage batteries charged up!

A cul-de-sac now runs through the station area. The enlarged feed mill and house (chimneys visible above the engine) provide the best links today. *R. A. Lumber/DHM*

CULMSTOCK: No 1450 passes over a level crossing as it enters the station on 24 February 1963 with the LCGB's 'Westcountryman Rail Tour'. The train had run from Waterloo to Exeter Central behind 60022 *Mallard*, and from there had been taken via Tiverton to Tiverton Junction by 2-6-2Ts Nos 4591 and 5564. The participants were then able to join this special working to Hemyock, the train being formed of the two regular branch coaches and five goods brake-vans. On returning to Tiverton Junction, the passengers rejoined the main train and were taken back to Paddington by *Mallard* (see page 106).

The Railway Hotel is situated just to the right of the photographer in the 'past' scene; now named the Culm Valley Inn, its car park occupies the site of the station. A footpath follows the formation through the gate in the left background. *Derek Frost/DHM*

WHITEHALL HALT: A public siding opened here with the line, but the halt did not open until 27 February 1933 when the GWR was attempting to develop business on the branch. The siding, long enough for three wagons, is on the left as the rail tour passes by. With a line speed of 15mph, the photographer had experienced no difficulty in getting ahead of the train again! By this time the ex-Barry coaches had been replaced by two ex-LNER vehicles due to difficulties in maintaining gas supplies. The 0-4-2Ts monopolised branch services for almost 30 years.

The grassed-over platform survives to this day. All of the 'present' pictures on this line were taken on 8 May 2005. *Derek Frost/DHM*

HEMYOCK: The terminus of the 7½-mile-long line is pictured on 7 September 1963 as the final passenger train, the 6pm to Tiverton Junction, departs behind No 1421. Typically, the train is 'mixed', with two loaded milk tanks in the consist. A pioneering butter producer had started operations here in the 1880s and ten years later acquired a feed mill across the road from the station to expand activities. United Dairies later acquired the business and concentrated on milk collection. This business developed over the years and provided much of the branch's income.

Grain and milk traffic ensured the line's survival, but by 1975 the only remaining business was fuel oil for the milk factory, the closure of which in October 1975 sealed the fate of the branch. The station site was about to be developed for housing in 2005. *R. A. Lumber/DHM*

Tiverton branch

HALBERTON HALT was the only intermediate station on this 4¾-mile-long line; it did not open until 5 December 1927 and was located about halfway along the branch. The line had been laid as broad gauge with provision for doubling the track in the future; accordingly overbridges were built with a wide span, and this halt was built beneath one that carried a road to the village of Halberton to the north. No 1450 is propelling its auto-coach as it leaves with the 3.35pm service from Tiverton Junction to Tiverton on 26 September 1964, one week before the last passenger trains ran. It will shortly pass under an aqueduct carrying the Grand Western Canal over the line.

A visit in May 2005 shows that the formation has been assimilated into a field. In the distance an overgrown cutting survives, but the lane on the left is the best link. *R. A. Lumber/DHM*

TIVERTON: When the line opened in June 1848 the terminus was provided with two platforms covered with a wooden overall roof. With the arrival of the Exe Valley Railway in 1885 a new station was built to suit its new junction status. Further building work in 1931 resulted in a new bay platform being provided for Tiverton Junction trains. This was not needed on 4 May 1964 as No 1442 waits with the 11.40am service to Tiverton Junction in the main up platform, as the Exe Valley line had already closed. This service, known locally as the 'Tivvy Bumper', will also cease in the following October, although freight services lasted until June 1967.

As seen in May 2005 a relief road called 'Great Western Way' now runs through the site of the station. No 1442 has survived, however, and can be found in Tiverton Museum. *R. A. Lumber/DHM*

Exe Valley Railway

BRAMPFORD SPEKE HALT: A standard gauge line from Tiverton to Stoke Canon was built by the GWR and came into use on 1 May 1885. This station was situated in the Exe flood plain, less than a mile from the junction at Stoke Canon and separated from its village by the river. Opening with the line as a full station, it was downgraded in status to that of an unmanned halt in 1923. Pictured from an adjacent occupation crossing, No 1451 is calling with the 5.48pm Exeter St David's to Dulverton train on 10 June 1963.

Today a public footpath passes over the site of the crossing, but unfortunately a not very inspiring view is to be had, even though both the main station building and house are occupied as separate dwellings. *Derek Frost/DHM*

BURN HALT FOR BUTTERLEIGH was opened on 26 January 1929 with the intention of serving an agricultural area. Burn itself comprises a single farm, while the small village of Butterleigh is more than 2 miles away. The halt was little used, a situation not helped by its proximity to the A396 and a regular bus service. Latterly only six peak services were scheduled to stop here. Just south of the halt, near Chitterley, No 1442 is propelling an auto-trailer forming the 6.10pm service from Bampton to Exeter on 10 June 1963.

As photographed on 8 May 2005, fencing still follows the line of the railway fence, but on the other side of the hedge the formation is now part of the field. *Derek Frost/DHM*

CADELEIGH was one of the original stations, when it was named 'Cadeleigh and Bickleigh', but the suffix was dropped in 1906 due to there being a Bickleigh station on the GWR's Launceston branch. The level of Sunday service on this line varied over the years and it was withdrawn totally in 1940 and not re-instated until the summer of 1950. On 30 September 1951 the last Sunday down train of the year is pictured from the main Exeter to Tiverton road as it departs.

Due to tree growth, a slightly more head-on view was selected on 8 May 2005 to show that a road now follows the formation and under the A396 bridge. It leads to an overflow car park for both the Devon Railway Centre, and the adjacent Bickleigh Mill. *R. A. Lumber/DHM*

CADELEIGH: At the north end of the station on Saturday 10 August 1963 No 1451 leaves with the 3.30pm Exeter St David's to Dulverton train.

After closure the site became a highways depot for Devon County Council, with the main buildings used as stores. The station was sold in 1997 and the Devon Railway Centre has been developed. Standard gauge track was re-laid between the platforms and Mk 1 coaches were obtained to house 15 model railway layouts. Among the other attractions are miniature and 2-foot-gauge railways. Kerr Stuart-built Pixie (No 4260 of 1922) was in use during the summer of 2005, and was pictured on 29 May. It was used for many years at the DCC's Wilminstone Quarry, near Tavistock. *R. A. Lumber/DHM*

COVE HALT: The northern section of this line from Tiverton to Morebath Junction came into use on 1 August 1884, thus pre-dating the southern part by nine months. A siding was provided at this hamlet, 2 miles south of Bampton, from the outset. A ballast-level halt was opened on 9 June 1924, to be replaced a few years later by a more substantial affair, including a typical GWR pagoda-style waiting shelter, the only one on the line. No 1450 is leaving with the 3.20pm Bampton to Exeter train on 15 June 1963.

Behind the camera is a level crossing complete with a crossing-keeper's cottage and adjoining signal cabin. These survive today as a dwelling, but a copse has grown on the site of the halt. The platform does survive beneath the growth – the ramp is the shadowed area beneath the tree on the left. *Peter W. Gray/DHM*

BAMPTON was the largest place on the northern section of the line, but still only a small market town, renowned for its annual Exmoor Pony Fair. No 1451 is heading the 1.10pm train from Dulverton to Exeter St David's on 8 July 1959. The line passing under the engine and away to the right leads to the goods yard, from where a siding ran to a limestone quarry that provided traffic for the railway from 1898 to about 1950.

This line closed on 7 October 1963 and the station area was subsequently largely infilled, with a car park and children's play area created. The 8 June 2005 view was taken a little further forward to show the trees and the building on the right, thus linking the two photos, rather than stand in a section of the cutting that exists behind the camera and from which the view is totally meaningless! *Peter W. Gray/DHM*

LOWER LODFIN CROSSING: From Bampton the line climbed at 1 in 66 through the steep valley of the Shuttern Brook for over a mile before reaching this level crossing. The gates are just visible to the right of the crossing-keeper's house as 0-6-0PT No 9629 approaches with the 2.08pm Exeter to Dulverton train on 8 July 1959. After passing over the crossing, the train will start to curve towards Morebath Junction, half a mile away, where it will join the Taunton to Barnstaple line.

The house is now occupied privately with its signal box used as a summer house. Situated in a delightful location, it is unfortunately largely obscured by trees in this June 2005 view. The trackbed can, however, be noted heading to the south. *Peter W. Gray/DHM*

INDEX OF LOCATIONS